Read All About Numbers

NUMBERS AND
SPEED

John M. Patten, Jr., Ed.D.

The Rourke Corporation, Inc.
Vero Beach, Florida 32964

John M. Patten, Jr. Ed.D.
25 years of professional experience as a writer, elementary and secondary school teacher, elementary school principal and K-12 system wide director of curriculum.
    B.A.—English and social studies; M.ED.—Guidance and education; ED.D.—Education

MATH CONSULTANT:
Mrs. Barbara Westfield, M.S. — Grade Three Teacher

PHOTO CREDITS
Cover, pages 4, 6, 15, 16, 21 Courtesy of Corel; pages 7, 8, 9 © John Patten; page 12 © M. Westerville, U.S. Fish and Wildlife service; page 21 © Zack Thomas

Library of Congress Cataloging-in-Publication Data

Patten, J. M., 1944-
    Numbers and speed / by John M. Patten, Jr.
        p. cm. — (Read all about numbers)
    Includes index.
    Summary: Describes some of the ways we measure how fast animals, people, vehicles, light and other things move.
    ISBN 0-86593-436-3
    1. Speed—Measurement—Juvenile literature. [1. Speed—Measurement.]
    I. Title II. Series: Patten, J. M., 1944- Read all about numbers
QC137.5.P37 1996
531.'3—dc20   96–12625
                                                                   CIP
                                                                    AC

Printed in the USA

TABLE OF CONTENTS

HOW FAST DO THINGS GO?

Snails and land turtles are not fast. Cars on a racetrack and wind in a storm are fast. How fast?

Are dogs faster than cats? How fast can people run?

Let's read about speed and how fast some things in our world can go.

Running an exciting race in Spain.

MEASURES AND SPEED

How fast something moves is a measure called **speed** (SPEED). Speed measures or tells how fast—like age tells how old and height tells how tall.

Age is told in measures of time like weeks or years. A child whose age is seven is called a seven-year-old.

Speed is how fast something moves.

Mph means miles per hour.

Heights are often in feet or miles. Mount Everest, the world's tallest mountain, is 29,028 feet high.

Everyday speeds are usually said in miles per hour (mph). Slower speeds can be feet per hour (fph). A few very fast things can go miles per second (mps).

NUMBERS AND SPEED

Numbers are used to tell speed. Slower things have smaller numbers and things that go fast have big numbers.

Cars, trains, and planes zoom along at fast speeds. Light goes so fast people can't even see it moving.

Other things, like the big hands on a clock or shadows on the ground, move slowly. They're moving but they seem to just stand still.

A rocket like this can zoom into the sky.

0
10
20
30
40
50
60
70
80
90
100
110
120
130
140
0
20
40
60
80
100
120
140
160
180
200
220
025929
km/h
mph

WAYS WE MEASURE SPEED

People have made different instruments, or gauges, to measure speed. They tell how fast something is moving.

A **speedometer** (speh DOM eh ter) shows how fast a bicycle, car, boat, plane or other vehicle is going. People walking or running can wear a **pedometer** (peh DOM eh ter) to find out their speed for a certain distance.

Traffic police use **radar** (RAY dahr) to see that cars and trucks on our roads obey safe speed limits. Weather reporters have **anemometers** (an eh MOM eh terz) that measure wind speeds from gentle breezes to hurricane gusts. Sometimes, in high winds, the anemometer blows away.

A speedometer like this tells how fast a car is going.

WHAT'S FAST AND WHAT'S NOT?

The cheetah, the world's fastest animal, can run 60 mph for short distances. Some antelopes can run 40 mph for over four miles. Most pet dogs are faster than pet cats.

On the other hand, the sloth, an animal that lives in Central America, drags itself along at only six to eight feet a minute. Take your ruler and measure how slow the sloth really is.

The cheetah is the world's fastest land animal.

Some spiders can run ten miles per hour.

The garden snail, if he doesn't stop for a rest, goes about 24 inches in three minutes. Many spiders are real speedsters, able to run at 10 mph, while some turtles, called tortoises, go only 10 feet in a minute.

The fastest fish, the bluefin tuna, swims through the ocean at speeds up to 60 mph; but the sea otter's top speed is 6 mph. A hummingbird can flap its wings as fast as 70 times each second.

FAST HUMANS

The speeds people can run are slower than the cheetah or antelope. A man has gone 27 mph and a woman, 23 mph.

The greatest distance a man has run in an hour is about 13 miles. The world's speed record for the marathon, a 26 mile footrace, is two hours and 10 minutes.

Now this is interesting: The fastest known talker spoke over 500 understandable words in a minute. Try that!

This runner looks very fast.

FAST VEHICLES

The fastest known speed for a car on a racetrack is 257 mph. The land speed record is 470 mph, set by a special vehicle powered by a rocket engine.

Modern highspeed trains reach speeds near 200 mph. Some big racing motorcycles go 185 mph. Air-cushion boats skim above the water at 75 mph on a calm day.

The jumbo jet can carry 500 passengers at 600 mph. A United States Air Force jet can fly at a fantastic 2,185 mph.

Motor racing is very exciting.

FAST, FAST WEATHER

The speeds of winds in storms can be very high and cause damage. Winds in a hurricane blow from 74 mph to 200 mph.

The two fastest windspeeds ever measured were 231 mph at the top of Mount Washington in New Hampshire and 284 mph in a tornado, or violent windstorm, in Texas.

Strong hurricane winds batter the shore and trees.

Cloud-to-ground lightening lights up the night sky over a city.

Cloud-to-ground lightening travels up to 930 mph on the way down from the sky. It goes even faster on the way back.

In tornadoes, winds near the center blow about 30 mph. Winds at the outer edges often reach a speed of 200 mph or more.

MORE INTERESTING SPEEDS

Some baseball pitchers can throw a baseball over 100 mph. Tennis balls can come off the racquet face at speeds over 135 mph.

The **speed of sound** (SPEED ov SOWND) is 1,100 feet per second. Sometimes people can see faraway things happen before they hear the sound from them—because light goes faster than sound.

The fastest known speed is the **speed of light** (SPEED ov LITE). Light travels 186,282 miles every second. Light is so fast, in outer space it goes a distance of almost six million miles a year.

A tennis ball can be hit 135 miles per hour.

GLOSSARY

anemometer (an eh MOM eh ter) — measures wind speeds

pedometer (peh DOM eh ter) — measures walking or running

radar (RAY dahr) — measures speed of cars or trucks on the road

speed (SPEED) — how fast something moves

speed of light (SPEED ov LITE) — 186,282 miles per second

speedometer (speh DOM eh ter) — shows how fast a bicycle, car, boat, plane, or vehicle is going

speed of sound (SPEED ov SOWND) — 1,100 feet per second

The speed of light is 186,282 miles per second.

INDEX